Sound Stewardship

Sound Stewardship:
How Shall Christians Think about Music?

Second Edition

Karen A. DeMol

Dordt College Press

Cover by Rob Haan
Layout by Carla Goslinga

Copyright © 2016 by Karen A. DeMol

Printed in the United States of America.

Dordt College Press   www.dordt.edu/DCPcatalog
498 Fourth Avenue NE
Sioux Center, Iowa 51250

ISBN: 978-1-940567-16-7

The Library of Congress Cataloging-in-Publication Data is on file with the Library of Congress, Washington, D.C.
Library of Congress Control Number: 2016949330

I am grateful that *Sound Stewardship* has been found to be helpful by many students, colleagues, and music-lovers. This second edition is not a revision, but an expansion and, I hope, a refinement. It has been prompted by responses from readers and by deepened insights gained from recent writings by others. To all these companions on the journey to understand and to serve in God's world – students, colleagues, music-lovers, scholars – I am deeply grateful.

Karen A. DeMol, Ph.D
Professor of Music *Emerita*, Dordt College
July 2016

TABLE OF CONTENTS

Introduction

As someone has said, "Nobody *doesn't* like music." Take a moment to consider the wide range of human experiences that music accompanies and enhances. Think of the number and the range of experiences in just one day that might be engaged with music. We may begin the morning by singing in the shower or listening to cheerful early morning music on the radio, bright brass perhaps. At work music makes our tasks more pleasant or even more efficient. We whistle or hum as we go about our daily activities, or have recorded music in the background, or use songs that help to coordinate physical motion. At dinner we may sing hymns as part of family devotions. We sing happy birthday to a chortling two-year-old, tucking her into bed with lullabies afterwards. At an evening sports event we might sing the school *Alma Mater* or the national anthem. We might relax at the piano or engage in an activity that is partnered by music, dancing perhaps, or skating, or watching a film. Or we might listen to great masterpieces of music on the stereo or live in concert. Yes, music is a common and a rich part of everyday life.

Music is also a part of every stage of life. Small children sing, crooning sing-song tunes of their own making, chanting to themselves of the day's events, and singing the childhood songs of their culture. Young lovers have "their song." Mature artists perform on the concert stage. Aged saints, past talking, sing life-giving Psalms. Music is also part of every culture. It is prominent in both the folk art and the "high art," the treasured masterpieces, of a culture. And all cultures use music in worship.

No, enjoying music and finding generous place for it in our lives is not a problem. But when we seek to articulate a Christian perspective on music, we can get caught short. How, exactly, does this wonderful world of music fit into a

Christian understanding of the world and of our place and task in it? How should we engage in music as part of our lives as Christians? How are we to evaluate music? What on earth does "giving glory to God" really mean when it comes to music? Christians have sought to understand all areas of life as being under the Lordship of Jesus Christ and in relation to the overarching realities of Creation, Fall, and Redemption, and the Eschaton. That approach provides a sound foundation for our understanding of music. In what follows, I present an overview of the implications of these great realities for music, though I realize it is impossible to explore fully their enormous implications for any particular aspect of life.

The four themes of Creation, Fall, Redemption, and Eschaton also help us keep our heads and our practice straight in a world where we are challenged both by those who do not believe any of these realities and also by our own inclination to stress redemption, but not creation, to emphasize salvation in the world to come, but not the reality of God's Kingdom now. A sound view of music should be based on creation and kingdom as well as on salvation. For our world belongs to God, in the beginning, now, and in the future!

These four themes and their implications for our activity in music are rich and deep. What follows is brief and basic, and will not reach their breadth and their depth. But it has been informed by "a cloud of witnesses," colleagues and students and also authors who have addressed the issues of this essay more extensively and deeply. The copious quotations and footnotes are intended not only to acknowledge sources, but also to deepen the thinking of the reader and to provide sources for further reading, while keeping this text succinct. The reader is strongly encouraged to consider the wealth of thought in the works listed in the bibliography.

Creation

The foundation of our activity in music is the creation. "In the beginning," Genesis 1–2 tells us, God by his Word called into being all that is. The Genesis list of created things is familiar to us – light, the waters, land, plants and trees, sun, moon, and stars, day and night, sea creatures, birds, and animals. This catalog of God's marvelous works is comprehensive, but it is not complete.

In the beginning: God's gifts in creation

Not specifically mentioned in Genesis but surely made by God are color, fragrance, flavor, texture, gravitational forces, the speed of light. No man made these wonders! Also not specifically mentioned in Genesis but surely made by God are the materials of which music can be made: sound itself, including sound waves, the overtone series, the resonating properties of larynx, wood, metal, and reed. God created the properties of sound and determined the physical laws governing the transmission of sound. God also created time. And God pronounced it all "good." "Good" here means perfect in the sense of being without flaw and also in the sense of being complete and satisfactory. "Good" also means having worth or value. God's creations are good "as is." Color is good! Sound is good! However, they also can be made into other things, and in the cultural mandate, God commanded us to do so. Clay is good "as is" and can also be shaped into pottery; vines are good "as is" and can also be made into rope and baskets; sound is good "as is" and can also be formed into language and music.

The raw materials of music – pitch, resonance, time – were created by God. When we work in music, we thus work within the givens of creation; no one makes music with raw materials other than these. That we are entrusted with these materials, materials declared good, materials with rich potential for development, should lead us to worshipful awe and grateful response. That we work within their limits should lead us to acknowledge humbly our creatureliness and finiteness.

God not only created but also sustains his world. Were he to stop, the overtone series would collapse into chaos and our voices fade to nothing. This is not a random universe, nor one run by a capricious God, but one sustained by a constant and faithful Maker. Musicians can trust that, because of his sustenance, the materials of sound will not change. Our energies need not be taken up by testing each morning whether the properties of sound are still the same, but can be concentrated on making good use of those properties. More good cause for gratitude!

Understanding what God did and did not provide at creation is important for the understanding of certain issues regarding music. First of all, did God create music or did he rather create the raw materials for music, leaving the development of music in human hands? If music is the *intentional shaping of sound*,[1] then understanding Creation shows us that, even though there are generous hints of music in nature – hints of rhythm in thunder and ocean wave and of melodic mottos in bird song, for instance – God did not create music. Rather, he created the raw materials and enabled humans to imagine ways of making them into music. The development of music is something done by humans, an activity possible only by humans, and a human responsibility encompassed in the cultural mandate. Composing and performing music is essentially a *human* activity. Some may say that "music is a great gift of God"; others may assert that "God gave me this song." We can admire the gratitude and humility in statements like these; we recognize the possibility of divine inspiration

---

1   Recent research about intentionality in bird and animal sounds may affect future thinking about this issue.

and realize that all good things ultimately come from God's hand. However, we ought to be clear that it is the potential for music, the raw materials – the overtone series, the resonating qualities of larynx, wood, and metal – that are the great gifts of God, as is our ability to shape something with them. Music itself is a cultural product, something humankind has made with the materials God provides. Music is a conscious and deliberate (and therefore creaturely) shaping of sound, for which we are responsible. A worrisome consequence of asserting that music in general or a specific piece is a direct gift or creation of God is that music is then set beyond criticism – how could we dare to critique a song if the composer was God? Such a claim becomes a barrier to the discerning and judging necessary in a world with both musical trash and musical masterpieces. On this matter William Edgar provides valuable insight, contrasting in depth the biblical view of culture and the views of culture found in other religions, ancient and modern, and of philosophers, such as Rameau and Rousseau. He writes, for example: "The first thing we learn from the much neglected fourth chapter of Genesis, then, is that music-making is human activity. The ancient world believed otherwise." And, "The problem, then, with finding a 'rival' source of music in nature is not that there is no music there, at least in some sense, but that we forget music's creatureliness, and man's crucial role as primary agent in the development of the musical process. Nature does not generate music independently from man, or from human agency (or angelic agency)." [2]

We should also note that music is physical; it is made of the materials of creation, made by our earthly bodies and produced with instruments made of created substances. We must take care not to think music super-human or to "spiritualize"

---

2   William Edgar, "Jubal's Bequest," *Taking Note of Music* (London: SPCK, 1986), 24, 29.

it or to put it on a supernatural pedestal – traps easy to fall into because of music's power to move and, perhaps, because of music's age-old association with the rites of worship. Music is as much a human activity as carpentry and photography, as playing and cooking.[3]

Then we should note that God called all that he made good. *All.* Time, out of which rhythm is made, is God's good gift. The resonating qualities of the wood out of which violins and clarinets can be made is good, and the resonating qualities of the human larynx are good. That would seem to suggest that both vocal/choral music and instrumental music are valid, and not to be prioritized. Instrumental music is different from vocal music, but it is not inferior just because it has no words.

Another understanding from creation is that God modeled for us amazing richness and diversity. In lavish, overflowing, joyful creativity, he created amusing armadillos and somber dachshunds, waddling penguins and delicate butterflies, elegant roses and sturdy redwoods, lemon yellow and deep purple, rough mountains and smooth lakes. His variety shows us that a rich diversity of design is valid. Although different styles may be appropriate for different contexts, and although not all styles may be appropriate for all contexts, we need not seek a single "ordained" musical style, nor hesitate to explore and enjoy new sounds and styles in music.[4] We may revel extensively in God's garden of sound![5]

---

3   Nicholas Wolterstorff, in *Art in Action: Toward a Christian aesthetic* (Grand Rapids: Eerdmans, 1980), writes, "Man's *embeddedness* in the physical creation, and his creaturely *vocation* and creaturely *end* within that creation, are where we must begin if we are to describe how the Christian sees the arts" (68–69).

4   The term "music" here includes all music – not only "art" or high art" music but also folk music, popular music, etc. For a discussion of music as art and as high art, see Edgar (45–47) and Wolterstorff.

5   "When musicians arrange tones and rhythms to reveal their interrelatedness,

Human created-ness and God's world of sound

Into this garden of delights, God placed us. What are the God-given characteristics of humankind that relate to music? First, let us rejoice that he made us with mouths and lungs to sing and to power wind instruments. Let us rejoice that he made us with ears – ears not only to hear each other speak, but also to hear the rustle of leaves, the growl of thunder, the purr of kittens – ears to hear the sounds of creation, ears to hear the music to be made out of the materials given in creation, as well as minds to appreciate them.

God also endowed us with creativity, the ability to imagine, to "think up" things, and to make them. All of us have this ability to some degree, while some of us are uniquely gifted in specific areas. But none of us can create out of nothing. Rather, we all work with the raw materials that God provided in his creation.

In our creativity we realize that we are dependent creatures in that we need other people and community for support, for ideas, and for the benefit of others' gifts. "It is not good for man to be alone" applies to our creative work too. Our work in music stands on the shoulders of musicians both around us and preceding us. Mozart and Beethoven could not write their intricate harmonies without the work of those in the Middle Ages who first began to write music in parts. They, in turn, could not weave melodic lines together without the work of those who first devised a system to codify and notate melody. Musicians thus work in community, both local and historical. The concept of community is built into our hu-

---

their potential for harmony, and their potential as materials for design, they glorify a Creator so wise that he could endow sounds with such properties, and so good that he placed his human creatures in a world that contains these sounds." Paul Munson and Joshua Farris Drake, *Art and Music: A student's guide* (Wheaton: Crossway, 2014), 84–85.

manness; its best expression is in the Body of Christ, with its acknowledged and celebrated dependence of all parts on each other.

Another important part of our created-ness is this: Every person is created with an aesthetic dimension – an ability to appreciate nuance, expressiveness, and beauty. Although "aesthetic" is hard to define, it includes the ability to perceive and appreciate balance, order, and expressiveness in the things we see and hear. It includes, but is not limited to, the appreciation of beauty.[6] This capability must be both recognized and nourished. Just as we care for ourselves and for others nutritionally and spiritually, so we must do aesthetically.[7] Although innate ability to perceive aesthetic qualities may differ from person to person, and although other duties do compete for our time, attention, and resources, none of us may set aside the development of our aesthetic sensitivities and skills. Even though some people are especially gifted in this area, all people can discern and enjoy/appreciate the aesthetic qualities of God's creation and the aesthetic qualities of things that others make of God's materials.

The gifts of creativity and aesthetic appreciation are not limited to believers. They are part of human nature created by God and are negated neither by the fall nor by unbelief. Even though the world has been tainted by sin, the aesthetic aspect of humankind and the ability to make things and to respond imaginatively within creation continues to be part of the calling that holds for believers and unbelievers alike. This

---

6   "Beauty" is itself a difficult concept to define. But however it is defined, the scope of music and other arts is much broader than "beauty."

7   Calvin Seerveld, in *Rainbows for the Fallen World* (Toronto: Tuppence Press, 1980), expresses this thought strongly: "An obedient aesthetic life is a matter of sanctification and not exactly a matter of heaven or hell" (61), yet people need "to find the way of the Lord for the aesthetic dimensions of our daily lives;" for "*aesthetic obedience* is required of everyone by the Lord" (9).

is of enormous importance as Christians consider whether they may listen to music written or performed by non-Christians. Giving thanks to God, we may indeed enjoy music by non-Christians, acknowledging that their gift is from God and that the materials of sound they work with are from God's good creation; at the same time, we need to discern what is misdirected about their work, as well as about our own.

The cultural mandate and its implications for activity in music

God not only created the materials and the ability to be imaginative, but he also gave a charge to develop them. In making man and woman, God decreed, "Let us make mankind in our image, in our likeness, so that they may rule over the fish in the sea and the birds in the sky, over the livestock and all the wild animals, and over all the creatures that move along the ground" (Genesis 1:26). After their creation, God blessed them with the commandment to be in charge: "God blessed them and said to them, 'Be fruitful and increase in number; fill the earth and subdue it. Rule over the fish in the sea and the birds in the sky and over every living creature that moves on the ground'" (Genesis 1:28). God blessed us thus!

We have a mandate, then, from God to be the cultivators of the good things of his creation. Our activity in any area is thus in response to having been charged with this task. That charge entails developing a culture.[8] Believers, knowing-

---

8 Richard T. Wright, in *Biology Through the Eyes of Faith* (San Francisco: Harper and Row, 1989), writes, "God has given us the responsibility of developing a culture, of learning to use the creation responsibly to form a human society that will express all of the good potential that exists in both the human mind and in the creation" (47). "These tasks – subduing, having dominion, cultivating – all point to the development of a culture. And since all of this is God's clear intention for humankind, the term *cultural mandate* has been used to describe this most basic of human responsibilities before God. We have a mandate from God to be the cultivators of the good things of his cre-

ly, and unbelievers, unknowingly, alike are busy at this work. Developing sound – part of the creation that God called "very good" – is included in this charge. Sound is part of the creation that God put us in charge of, to care for, to explore, and to develop.[9]

We call this a "task" – but what a task! Genesis says God *blessed* them with this task. Not a burden, but a joy. What a gift – to be let loose in a garden of great wonders and delights and of enormous potential and to be told by God himself to "play" in it. "It's all good," he said, "very good! See for yourself! See what you can make of it now. Have a good time at it! And remember – you are accountable to me."

Of course no one is able fully to respond to all aspects of creation; no one of us has either time enough or the specific gifts fully to explore and develop every aspect of creation. Even in regard to just one aspect of creation – sound – there are various "specialists" who respond in different ways. Physicists develop the understanding of the nature of sound. Technicians develop the measurement of sound (as with clocks and oscilloscopes, tuners and metronomes) and the harnessing of sound (as with public address systems and radio and recording technology). Musicians respond to sound by developing its aesthetic possibilities, shaping it for expressive purposes. In fact, music can be defined as an aesthetic response to creation

---

ation. This mandate means that God has intended for humankind to interact with his creation in such a way that we would develop a culture. In doing so, we use the created elements and so demonstrate clearly our dominion" (169). See also Brian J. Walsh and J. Richard Middleton, *The Transforming Vision: Shaping a Christian world view* (Downers Grove: InterVarsity, 1984) and Albert M. Wolters, *Creation Regained: Biblical basics for a reformational worldview*, 2nd ed. (Grand Rapids: Eerdmans, 2005).

9 "When musicians arranges tones and rhythms to reveal their interrelatedness, their potential for harmony, and their potential as materials for design, they glorify a Creator so wise that he could endow sounds with such properties, and so good that he placed his human creatures in a world that contains these sounds." Munson and Drake, 84–85.

in the area of sound.[10]

In sum, we, made with an aesthetic dimension to our being and an ability to create, are called to live in a world in which sound has been made by God himself and declared very good. God has set us in charge of both keeping and developing his world of sound, as well as the rest of creation. Music-making is thus a part of our humanness and part of our task in God's world.

Various elements of music are responses to specific elements of creation. Rhythm, which includes tempo, meter, and the duration of notes, is an aesthetic response to or development of time, the *temporal* and *sequential* aspect of creation. Melody and harmony (uses of pitch) are aesthetic responses to or development of the aspect of sound called *frequency* (high and low pitches). Dynamics are aesthetic responses to or development of the property of sound called *amplitude* or *volume* (the ability of sound to be loud or soft, with any number of gradations in between). Tone color or *timbre* is an aesthetic response to or development of the timbral or resonance qualities of materials such as wood, metal, skin. All people at all times and in all places and in all cultures still have all of these and only these aspects of music to work with. We have all of these – a rich supply of materials; and we have only these – we work within their limits. Every time I read a new music appreciation book or a world music book, I find it begins with a chapter on the materials of music; the materials discussed in every book are rhythm, melody and harmony, dynamics, and tone color; and they are all directly tied to elements of creation.

In addition, music obeys the command to develop creation by molding musical order and musical shape. In fact,

---

10 Edgar defines music as "*human, cultural activity, ordered by the covenant, in the aspect of sound*" (45).

music can be defined as the deliberate or conscious organization of sound, in contrast to noise. There are of course no direct models in creation for specific musical designs such as minuets or twelve-bar blues. However, music is engaged in configuring order and design, as are all the arts. In music we continue God's work of developing order in his creation.

Over the long centuries and in all places and cultures of the world, people have responded to sound in God's creation in an amazing variety of types and styles of music, from the improvisatory groupings of melodic and rhythmic fragments of the East and the rhythmic intricacies of Africa to the highly harmonic styles of Europe, from childhood songs to worship music, from chants and folk songs to symphonies, with voices, percussion, wind, and string instruments – a lavish, rich, diverse display.[11]

The Fall

To our grief, human sin in the Fall and in our daily lives ever since has stained and warped everything. Sin's role in physical illness has produced not only cholera and cancer but also tinnitus and deafness. Sin spoils our ability to make good things, it interferes with our aesthetic perceptions and our enjoyment, it taints our motives, it confuses our ability to discern. We ourselves are sinful; our cultural products also, our responses to creation, are muddied both by our own sin

---

11 "God speaks one Word. A thousand cultures respond. 'In the beginning was the word...' Ever since, people have been responding to that Word through the art, music, and traditions of their cultures. Some cultures respond with primness, neatness, and order; some with exuberance, joy, and passion. Some respond more intellectually; others more emotionally. Some with prayer and fasting; others with hospitality and song. Out of that variety of responses, God creates a beautiful mosaic of color and motion, a unity out of diversity. Enjoy that mosaic; celebrate the color and motion; praise God for both the unity and the diversity." Synodical Committee on Race Relations advertisement, *The Banner* (July 1, 1991), 29.

and by sinful influences.[12] We may not want to believe that sin affects so abstract or so beloved a thing as music, but our music-making is not exempt from sin's long shadow. We can perceive its effects in music in a sad multitude of ways. In our engagement with music, which often focuses on the pleasure of music, we must not fail to discern these effects and seek to correct them both in our own lives and in our culture. Consider the following examples.

The *actual musical content* can be spoiled by sin. It is intriguing to conjecture what music sounded like before the Fall, but also futile, for we have no information at all. It is also impossible to know whether the Fall affected the basic created materials of music. For instance, could the overtone series have been different before the Fall? Was the resonance of wood richer? Did Adam and Eve have perfect pitch memory? We cannot know.

Surely, however, sin does affect the content of the music; I speak here specifically of the music itself, the words or lyrics being a separate, though often related, issue. We cannot say that "sins" exist in the "notes" of music as if they were moral sins, like embezzlement or gossip. An analogy with clothing is useful: various fibers, such as cotton and wool, are not sinful, but the way we assemble them can be, if we make them into clothing that is shabby or sloppy or seductive.[13] In music sinfulness shows up in the taint of mediocrity; music can be trite, shallow, shoddy, or redundant. Music can be poorly crafted, formulaic rather than imaginative, with run-of-the-mill melodies, trite harmonic variety, and unimaginative repetition.

---

12 Wright expresses it thus: "The very culture that we develop will also show the impact of the Fall; two forms of its expression will appear, reflecting the two kingdoms that are now at war – God's kingdom and Satan's. The entire range of human activities becomes a battleground, for there is nothing in the creation or culture that remains unaffected by sin" (171).

13 I am indebted to Jessica Boonstoppel for this helpful analogy.

It can carry weak, poorly constructed texts or texts with deceptive concepts. Music can be pretentious, which is related to dishonesty. Music can be crafted or used to manipulate, which is devious.

The mixture of influences is also evident in musical style. As an example of the dilemma, the music of Mozart and Haydn has superb qualities of orderliness and balance that reflect the orderliness of creation, but which also reflect the rationalism of the Enlightenment; it has grace and elegance, which reflect the beauty of unmarred creation, but it also reflects the aristocratic mannerisms of the French court.

Our *understanding of music* can be spoiled by sin. We can have too low a view of music, considering it outside the domain of Christian service and sanctification, or one to be "indulged" only when "more essential" areas of life are well in hand. This view is common in our culture, showing up, for example, in educational priorities. Or we can have too high a view of music, paradoxically also a strong trait in our culture. We can pridefully hold music-making to be a "higher" calling than, for instance, computer science or plumbing. We can consider music a badge of our superiority, either personally or culturally. We can "idolize" musicians; a tendency to do so began in the Western world in the nineteenth century, which regarded artists as extra-human, elevated, super-beings, and continues in our own time, with adulation both of rock stars and of concert artists. We can even idolize Christian artists, as if they are some sort of super-Christians. Artists themselves can "buy into" this attitude, displaying an unbecoming arrogance.

Our *aesthetic sense* has been spoiled by the fall. Our ability to appreciate and to discern aesthetic matters is hobbled. Further, it is difficult to distinguish whether our aesthetic capabilities are limited by sin, by differences of gifts, by human finiteness, or by a mixture of these. Certainly our culture flattens and deadens our aesthetic perceptions; our culture has even been called "aesthetically dysfunctional." Enabled by the resources of technology, our culture plays music so continuously and so pervasively that our ability to appreciate it and to be discerning is blunted.

We can also be lazy or not interested in learning discernment about music and the other arts. We are content to enjoy music in only a superficial way, rather than striving to appreciate the wonders of God's creation in it. We can desire immediate musical gratification instead of striving for excellence and refinement. Our music-making is handicapped when we do not try for our best, either in our practicing or in our attitude. We can fail or even refuse to use our God-given ability in music. In addition, physical impairments resulting from sin's brokenness handicap composers, performers, and listeners. Some of us have damaged our hearing, or even gone deaf. Others' finger dexterity has been crippled by arthritis. The pianist Leon Fleischer has lost the use of his right arm, while clarinetist Robert Marcellus went blind, no longer able to see the printed score.

Our *use of music* can be spoiled by sin. We can use music thoughtlessly, or engage in it in ways that humiliate others, or use it to fit social status to which we aspire. We can use music destructively; note the current warnings that the volume of much contemporary music is physically damaging to our hearing. We can use music too extensively; for example, our culture plays music so constantly in every situation that our ability to "hear" it is deadened – we have learned simply to tune it out. We can confuse the appropriate uses of music; for example, Neal Plantinga, writing of sin as pollution and perversion, points out that "when a church uses hymns primarily as entertainment, it simultaneously perverts the hymns and pollutes worship by introducing entertainment into it."[14]

Some misuses of music can appear mild and may be unintentional. But there have been uses of music that are egregious, intentionally hurtful, and humiliating. Any country or culture that intentionally suppresses valid expressions of music shows disrespect for its people. Who would do such a thing? Unfortunately there are horrid examples. In Nazi Germany, music by Jewish composers was first suppressed, then forbidden. Worse, music was used in service of the Nazi program to humiliate, subjugate, deceive, torment, and even to kill prisoners in concentration camps. Prisoners were forced to sing pro-Nazi and anti-Semitic songs, to play cheerful music to deceive those newly arriving at the camps, to "celebrate" the return of escapees, and to mask the screams of those being tortured; starved and weak prisoners were forced to sing while doing heavy labor to the point of dying from sheer exhaustion.[15] The aesthetic quality of the music selected is not the problem here; rather, it is the hideous use of music to harm, to demean, and to destroy that reveals the depths of sin in the use of what we would like to consider only a beautiful and pleasure-giving art.

Nearer in time and closer to home, it has been documented that one of the "enhanced interrogation techniques" designed by the USA as part of the Global War on Terror, intended to force prisoners to reveal important information, was subjecting prisoners to the extremely loud and unrelenting playing of Western music offensive to the prisoners (a

---

14 Cornelius Plantinga, Jr. *Not the Way It's Supposed to Be: A breviary of sin* (Grand Rapids: Eerdmans, 1995), 43.

15 Benita Wolters-Fredlund, "Hearing Hate: Revisiting Nazi music" Unpublished paper, July, 2011. Szymon Laks, a Polish musician who survived Auschwitz, details his first-hand experience with these horrors in *Music of Another World*, translated by Charles A. Kisiel (Evanston: Northwestern University Press, 1989).

"no touch" torture).[16] Professional musicians in the American Musicological Society, learning of this horror, protested – as we all must protest when anything in God's creation is used to wound and to break.

Yes, we must protest – *and* repent, for in all of our music-making, we fall short of the glory of God, and need his forgiveness and restoration.

Sin can infect music as it interacts with other fields as well. For example, when music is published, it legitimately interacts with business. However, an inordinate desire to make money can compromise or even dominate the music-making process, pressing musicians to compose or record what will sell rather than focusing on excellent aesthetic work. Unfortunately, music can be used merely as a tool to sell something, from beef and plane tickets to the Gospel itself.

And music can even become our god. In the words of a contemporary testimony, "we abuse the creation or idolize it."[17] How could music become a god? Surely we do not expect that music will save us! Yet if we believe music is what gives ultimate purpose or meaning to our lives, or if like some Romantics we consider artists to be some kind of super-human, or if we fail to acknowledge the God who is the source of all good gifts, we may have warped music into an idol.

Our original task stands: to guard and protect and to develop God's world of sound. But because of the Fall, we now must also become discerning about the implications of sin for music, counteract its effects, and restore an appropriate

16 Suzanne Cusick, "Music as Torture/Music as Weapon," *TRANS: Transcultural Music Review* 10 (2006) http:www.sibetrans.com/trans/trans10Cusck_eng.htm and "'You are in a place that is out of the world...' Music in the Detention Camps of the 'Global War on Terror,'" *Journal of the Society for American Music* 2/1 (February, 2008), 1–26.

17 *Our World Belongs to God: A contemporary testimony* (Grand Rapids: CRC Publications, 2008), par. 15.

understanding and use of music.

Redemption

But the great good news for us and for the marred creation is this: Christ through his atoning work has brought redemption. Music, part of all of life, and subject to all the ills of the Fall, is part of creation regained, part of the redeemed life. We now have even more cause to respond in gratitude, obedience, and service! "The man whose life has been saved by God responds, with patterned sounds, in the joy of thankfulness. This is more than pleasurable sensation. It places the emotional meaning of music, or rather its way of meaning, in the context of the covenant. To be sure, his heart is renewed by God's grace. . . . He can sing a 'new song' because he is a 'new person' in Christ."[18]

Believers, now both responding to the original cultural mandate and thanking God for salvation, are called to work as Christ's partners and agents in the renewal of the entire creation. Just as all of life falls under the cultural mandate, and just as all of life was contaminated by sin, so now all of life, having been redeemed by Christ, needs healing. We are called to be engaged in the restoration of God's broken world.

However, Christians have differing views on the importance of cultural activity since the fall and since Christ's redemptive sacrifice. Some Christians believe that the most urgent task is the saving of souls for the world to come, that this world and its culture is for the most part a "vale of tears" that will pass away. In this view, artistic activity would be legitimate if there had been no fall, but because of the fall and of the urgent need of humankind for knowledge of salvation, all Christians must be engaged either entirely or primarily in evangelism and missions. First things first. The arts count

18 Edgar, 68.

only as a tool for outreach.

For others, redemptive tasks fall in a hierarchy: missions and evangelism first, then works of healing, such as medicine and nutrition, with perhaps agriculture education for the Third World following close behind, then education; other areas, such as business, sports, the arts, and politics, are either at the bottom of the list or considered questionable turf for Christians.

Christians in the Reformed tradition, however, believe that this world and these already-not-yet times are part of the Kingdom of God. In fact, "the goal of redemption is nothing less than the restoration of the entire cosmos."[19] Evangelism can be understood as bringing God's good news to all areas of culture. The realities of the fall and of redemption neither erase the creation nor negate the cultural mandate.[20] "All legitimate vocations are holy in their own distinct way and even precede the specific calling of gospel ministry."[21]

If anything, there is now yet another reason for Christians to be busy in all areas of life. Through human sin, not only we humans, but also our entire planet Earth is marred. "The whole creation groans," says Paul. In every area of life – physical, moral, emotional, intellectual, social, and artistic

---

19 Michael Williams, "A Restorational Alternative to Augustinian Verticalist Echatology," *Pro Rege* 20:4 (June, 1992): 19.

20 See Edgar, Ch. 2. "Genesis 4 speaks against divinizing art, but it also speaks against secularizing it. Although the Fall has troubled man's pursuit of the original mandate of Genesis 1.28, it has not interrupted it, contrary to our first impressions" (33–34).

21 John Bolt, *Bavinck on the Christian Life.: Following Jesus in faithful service* (Wheaton: Crossway, 2015), 46. Also: "'[O]rdinary' vocations, rooted as they are in our created nature as image bearers of God 'ruling' over his world, actually precede the specific call of gospel ministry and kingdom service. The creation order, we noted, is prior to God's work of redemption.... *All* Christians who follow Christ in stewarding God's 'good and perfect gift[s] (James 1:17), in whatever vocation, are acting as responsible Christian disciples" (Bolt, 162–163).

– the whole creation groans, screeches, cracks notes as it were, plays out of tune, misses the beat. The whole creation – not our souls only – needs redemption.[22] Christ is Redeemer and King not only of our souls and for eternity, but also of human culture and for now. The task of the redeemed Christian is to proclaim the Good News of the Gospel both to unbelievers that they may swell the chorus in heaven, and also to our culture, that in its expressions and structures it may bring honor to God now.[23] We press the claims of Christ into all of life and into every area of culture: in the social structures that could oppress, the commercial ventures that could exploit, the illnesses that maim and kill, the artistic expressions that could debase. Polluted rivers are to be cleansed, disease conquered, artistic life cleansed, enriched, and marked by new integrity. Abraham Kuyper's famous statement that "there is not a square inch in the whole domain of our human existence over which Christ, who is sovereign over *all*, does not cry 'Mine!'" applies to music; we claim that there is not an inch of audio tape, or a measure of printed music, or a minute of performance, that does not fall under the lordship of Jesus Christ. In doing so we proclaim that this world counts, here and now, because God made it and because God redeems it.[24]

---

22 It is significant that one of God's covenants, the one after the flood, was with the animals as well as with Noah: "Then God said to Noah and to his sons with him, 'I now establish my covenant with you and with your descendants after you and with every living creature that was with you – the birds, the livestock, and all the wild animals, all those that came out of the ark with you – every living creature on earth. I establish my covenant with you. Never again will all life be cut off by the waters of a flood; never again will there be a flood to destroy the earth" (Genesis 9:8–11).

23 Cf. 1 Corinthians 10:23–11:1; 2 Corinthians 10:3–6.

24 Wright explains, "Our stewardly task is therefore extended beyond basic management and wise use; it now involves an opportunity to participate in this redemption by bringing healing to the creation and the restoration of goodness to the culture" (176).

Service/Task

How then shall we be engaged with music? First of all, with gratitude and delight – gratitude to God for the provision of the materials of music and his command to be busy with them, and delight in the good things musicians have made of them. Enjoying music is a blessed pleasure!

Then, we should engage in music to acknowledge and to nourish the aesthetic aspect of our created nature – a task that is both enjoyable and needed. We noted earlier that all people have an aesthetic dimension; attending to this aspect of ourselves and of our lives helps care for God's creation. Because music can provide us with such pleasure, it may seem too sober to call attending to our aesthetic life as part of a Christian's task; the "should" here may sound like a burden. Yet some people do need to be reassured that aesthetic activity is valid. In addition, the fallen nature of every area of life has made necessary the development of discernment. So as we enjoy music (as all of us do), we may – and should! – seek to enrich our enjoyment, and we should – and can! – develop our discernment in our musical choices. These tasks, if we may call them that, engage both musicians and musical lay-people in seeking to discern musical quality, to use music thoughtfully, and to recognize and work against distortion and evil when it occurs in music. According to Calvin Seerveld, this is part of sanctification, which includes more areas of life than we might think; while obedient aesthetic life is not exactly a matter of heaven or hell, it is part of sanctification – of being made holy to the Lord.[25]

We are all to be willing to be served in this endeavor by those uniquely gifted in music. Just as we look to those gifted and trained, say, in medicine, dietetics, and exercise for the wellbeing of our bodies, so we should look to those gifted and

---

25 Seerveld, 61.

trained in music and the arts to nurture our wellbeing in the aesthetic areas of life.[26]

Those who are uniquely gifted in any field are to be willing to develop their gifts and to use them for the building up of the Body of Christ. Practically speaking, this means that some of us will be busy in evangelism and some in pastoral work, some working in economics and some in agriculture, some in commerce and some in the arts.[27] The Christian community has long acknowledged the variety of gifts and talents, at least in concept.[28] In actuality, it sometimes has more difficulty with some fields of endeavor than with others. For example, some people have difficulty with the possibility or legitimacy of Christian activity in business or politics. Others consider the natural sciences dangerous, or the arts irrelevant

---

26 For rich discussions of service and of the musician's task, see Edgar, Ch. 5, and Wolterstorff, 192–199.

27 This discussion assumes the rightful place of work in the world. For a thorough discussion of what that "rightfulness" in the Christian life and in relation to salvation implies, see Bolt, Ch. 8, "Work and Vocation."

28 Edgar expands: "In the biblical view, everyone can sing, but not everyone belongs to the family of musicians. Everyone is called to participate in the enjoyment of music, but not everyone is qualified to be called a musician. This is not a kind of elitist privilege, but a genuine vocation, to be accomplished with skill and hard work" (36). Thus, he says, Jubal, who made musical instruments, is the father of *musicians*. "So calling attention to the instruments focuses on the specific art of music to be developed by those who belong to that family, in the same way that having cattle (4:20) focuses on those who belong to the family of herdsmen. All are not qualified in the same way. Adam could probably sing (2:23 is likely to be a song), but is not the father of every skill." Also, "Music, then, is a divine calling. Not in some mystical, individualistic way, but because of the structure of the cultural mandate" (36). "Music, insofar as it belongs to human, cultural activity, is a divine calling. Even fallen Adam could not escape his obligation as a culture-builder. Despite the pain of labor after the fall (3:17–19), despite the rebellious orientation of much of cultural activity (4:22–24), by God's grace, we are still called to build culture, to enjoy it, to exercise the functions outlined in the original mandate. Jubal's double apologetic is clear: music is human activity, but it is also a divine calling" (37).

or dangerous or both. We need to reaffirm that all areas are worthy fields of endeavor for Christians.[29]

As we seek wisdom in our view of gifts and service, we can be instructed by examples from Scripture that illustrate both the giving of design and crafting skill in the arts and the calling of those so gifted into the service of the community. At the construction of the Tabernacle, Moses said to the Israelites,

> See, the LORD has chosen Bezalel son of Uri, the son of Hur, of the tribe of Judah, and he has filled him with the Spirit of God, with wisdom, with understanding, with knowledge and with all kinds of skills – to make artistic designs for work in gold, silver and bronze, to cut and set stones, to work in wood and to engage in all kinds of artistic crafts. And he has given both him and Oholiab son of Ahisamak, of the tribe of Dan, the ability to teach others. He has filled them with skill to do all kinds of work as engravers, designers, embroiderers in blue, purple and scarlet yarn and fine linen, and weavers – all of them skilled workers and designers. So Bezalel, Oholiab and every skilled person to whom the LORD has given skill and ability to know how to carry out all the work of constructing the sanctuary are to do the work just as the LORD has commanded. (Exodus 35:30–36:1)

In another passage God refers to skilled craftsmen thus: "Have Aaron your brother brought to you from among the Israelites, along with his sons Nadab and Abihu, Eleazar and Ithamar, so they may serve me as priests. Make sacred garments for your brother Aaron to give him dignity and honor. Tell all the

---

29 "All legitimate vocations are holy in their own distinct way and even precede the specific calling of gospel ministry. God's act of creation and his creational, natural gifts to humanity all precede the redemption begun with the Call of Abraham…Christians who serve God by stewarding the use of his 'good and perfect' gifts – in the home, in Education, in medicine, in law, in business, in government, and so forth – are acting as responsible Christian disciples and should be honored for it. The notion of *Christian* discipleship should not be restricted to service that is explicitly linked to the gospel ministry, Christian witness, or Christian service. We live our Christian lives in the vocations to which God calls us, whatever they may be" (Bolt, 46–47).

skilled workers to whom I have given wisdom in such matters that they are to make garments for Aaron, for his consecration, so he may serve me as priest" (Exodus 28:1–3). And earlier in Exodus 26:1: "Make the tabernacle with ten curtains of finely twisted linen and blue, purple and scarlet yarn, with cherubim woven into them by a skilled worker."

Music too in the Old Testament had specific and demanding requirements and was under the direction of head musicians. The Tabernacle musicians, identified by name, "performed their duties according to the regulations laid down for them" (1 Chronicles 6:31–46). Specific individuals, who are listed by name and of whom Asaph was chief, were to play lyres and harps. In addition, "Asaph was to sound the cymbals, and Benaiah and Jahaziel the priests were to blow the trumpets regularly" (1 Chronicles 16:4–6, 42).[30]

These passages apply to worship. What about concert music, folk music, dance music? Because all of life is religious, in all its dimensions rooted in our relationship to God, God's servants today too must see that the gifts of creativity and skill given to artisans and musicians are to be recognized and put to use by the musicians and community alike in all areas of life where the arts come into play.

For the musicians themselves, the tasks can be summed up as threefold. One task relates to the cultural mandate: to make music and make it well, imaginatively developing the created domain of sound, in obedient, humble, and joyful response to the mandate to develop God's good world. In obeying this mandate, musicians seek both to honor God and to bring about something of benefit and delight to their fellow

---

30 In *Art for God's Sake* (Philipsburg, NJ: PR Publishing, 2014), Philip Ryken draws four fundamental principles for a Christian theology of the arts from these Exodus passages: the artists' call and gifts come from God; God loves all kinds of arts; God maintains high standards for goodness, truth, and beauty; art is for the glory of God (17 ff).

humans. Musicians are to choose and to write music of quality and integrity and to perform it well. They may choose to do so within familiar musical styles. But also, secure in the knowledge that the world of sound is God's world and that he himself was not timid in the diversity of his creations, musicians are free to strike out boldly into new styles as well. Artists who are Christians can be and should be in the forefront of musical creativity and authenticity.

That task alone could well take all the musicians' time and energy. But there is another task, too, one necessitated by the fall: to identify the distortions and evils relative to music and to work both to counteract them and to promote the good.

In both of these tasks musicians fulfill the third task: to serve the Body. As servants we are to make music not only in obedient and joyful response to God our Maker and Redeemer, but also in humble and loving service to our neighbor. We carry out our musical work in concern for our neighbor's wellbeing, because that is the way all God's gifts of talent and ability are to be used. For there is a splendid economy and a wonderful match: each person, created by God, has many aspects and many needs, including an aesthetic dimension to their being and aesthetic needs. Others have been gifted to meet and to serve those needs. These gifts have been given, not to mark us as superior, or to give us private pleasure, but to equip us for service. Artists are servants among servants. As the dietician tends to our nutritional needs and the physician to our medical needs, so the musician tends our aesthetic needs.

Serving demands both a servant's attitude and quality of service. It is true that the sincerity of the server's heart is important. It is also true that the serving heart will seek quality workmanship. Sincerity of heart does not excuse poor compositional craftsmanship, grating tone quality, poor tuning, and sloppy rhythms. As someone has said, "Holy shoddy is still shoddy." Yet, at the same time, without sincerity of heart, our most perfect music is but a "noisy gong." Aesthetic excellence and true service are mutually inclusive. Serving as a dietician means serving quality food. Serving as an automaker or mechanic means seeing to it that our neighbor's brakes do not fail. Serving as a musician means seeing to it that music does not fail our neighbor aesthetically. Serving as a musician means choosing to do that which builds our neighbor musically. Musicians do this by composing and performing music of high aesthetic quality, by choosing appropriate music for the many situations of life, and, in a world that includes both musical mediocrity and trash as well as musical greatness, by helping others to build discernment about musical quality.

Shalom

In all these endeavors in music we are working for a right understanding and a good practice of music, working in obedience to God's mandates, and working for *shalom*. Shalom is more than peace; it is wellness, wholeness, completeness, perfection, and security in every area of creation, in every area of personal, social, intellectual, and artistic life. And in the wellbeing of *shalom*, all areas of life are infused with joy; engagement in them is rich with rejoicing. *Shalom* is what we work toward now as we press God's claims over all of creation; it is what will be made perfect in the new earth, when the whole creation will be purified and made new.

Just what might *shalom* mean for music? We cannot now fully picture what such complete wholeness and perfection will be like in the new heaven and new earth. But we can imagine, and work now toward the development of music attuned to the original mandate to develop God's good world of sound, a use and development of music free from the handicaps and confusions of sin. In a culture of *shalom*, music will be an integral part of the whole of life, neither merely reserved for moments of high worship or high art concert life, nor regarded as optional or as frivolous entertainment. Music, never cheap or self-seeking or unthinkingly used, will be appropriate and of outstanding quality throughout this culture.

In a culture of *shalom* music will interact well with many other areas of life, and yet maintain its essential aesthetic integrity. In a culture of wholeness, music will be an integral part of and contributor to the health and wellbeing of every aspect of personal and communal life. In such a culture, by doing and being these things, music will truly be for the glory of God.[31]

And when *shalom* is made complete in the new heaven and new earth, what will music be like then? It is impossible for us now to imagine the music of the new heaven and new earth, but trying to do so can fill us with awe and excitement and anticipation. Isaiah foretells that "Then will the eyes of the blind be opened and the ears of the deaf unstopped. Then will the lame leap like a deer, and the mute tongue shout for joy. Water will gush forth in the wilderness and streams in the desert. The burning sand will become a pool, the thirsty ground bubbling springs. In the haunts where jackals once lay, grass and reeds and papyrus will grow. And a highway will be there: it will be called the Way of Holiness" (Isaiah 35:5–8a). Once again the earth will be perfect, unspoiled, harmonious. God and his people and his creation in perfect harmony! God's original creation perfectly restored! What earthbound words can guess at the splendor of that City of God? What

---

31 "Made in God's image to live in loving communion with our Maker, we are appointed earthkeepers and caretakers to tend the earth, enjoy it, and love our neighbors. God uses our skills for the unfolding and well-being of his world so that creation and all who live in it may flourish." *Our World Belongs to God: A contemporary testimony* (2008), par 10.

words hint at the glory of the music in that perfect place? It is beyond our greatest present imagination. And yet we can now imagine that then each piece – simple song or intricate symphony – will have its own perfect integrity. Form will align perfectly with function. "All God's children will have a place in the choir" – and with such voices, the voices of resurrected bodies! Those same bodies, never subject to fatigue, will be capable of astounding feats of bowing and double-tonguing, but will never do them just for show. Artistic imagination, too, will be free of all handicap, all distortion. And with nothing suspect, with jealousy eternally banished, and with every barrier to enjoyment gone, all musical efforts will be appreciated to the fullest. Will there still be diversity of talent? If so, no barriers will impede the full expression of that talent. Will there be diversity of style in this city to which "the kings bring in their cultures"[32]? If so, there will be no shabbiness; all the music will be perfectly well-shaped, balanced, and expressive. And all done to the glory of God and in joy by his people.

What a day that will be! This is the day, this coming time of *shalom*, to which our present lives must now point. "Our daily lives of service [now] aim for this moment" when "we will join in the new song to the Lamb without blemish, . . . righteousness and peace will flourish, everything will be made new, and every eye will see at last [and every ear will hear] that our world belongs to God!"[33] Amen! Come quickly, Lord Jesus!

Issues

What a day that will be! But that day is not yet, and in

---

32 For this understanding of Isaiah 60 and Revelation 21:24, see Richard Mouw, *When the Kings Come Marching In: Isaiah and the New Jerusalem*, revised edition (Grand Rapids: Eerdmans, 2002).

33 *Our World Belongs to God* (1986), par. 57 and 58.

this world now we face a variety of issues, important and challenging issues, even in the delightful world of music. We Christians seeking to bring all areas of this present life under the lordship of Christ encounter many questions either in our own minds or in the Christian culture at large. I hear these questions raised by students, by performers, by members of church music committees, by those deciding which radio stations to tune in to and which CDs to purchase. Is there a Christian musical style? What would make it so? May we listen to music by non-Christian performers or perform music by non-Christian composers? Can music lead people to believe (as is the hope with evangelistic music) or to sin (a common fear with rock and rap)? How does music carry meaning? How shall we evaluate music? And how shall we be guided to understand these concerns? Let us explore some of these current issues in light of the foundation set forth above.

How shall we understand the term "Christian music"?

The preceding discussion, with its emphasis on the great realities of creation and Kingdom, should factor into a Christian's comprehensive understanding of music. All of the above concerns "Christian music." Unfortunately, the term "Christian music" is currently in common use in a different sense. A common attitude or hope is that there is or should be a distinctively "Christian" kind of music; in the same vein, a common concern or fear surrounds using music composed or performed/recorded by non-Christians.

It seems to me that these are exactly the points where an awareness of the creation and our place in it can lead to a proper understanding of music. Let us restate that all humans are given the ability to shape things out of the materials of creation. Further, special gifts to be creative in certain areas are not limited to those who acknowledge God. Just as he sends rain on the just and the unjust, God endows both Christians and non-Christians with skills to make beautiful and useful music. We cannot say that all music written or performed by believers will be aesthetically better than that by unbelievers; believing is not a prerequisite for making aesthetically good music. The spiritual distinction between those who have faith in Christ and those who do not does not result in two distinctly different types of music, Christian and non-Christian. Because both believers and unbelievers work with the materials given in creation, they will both work within the givens of the overtone series, the principles of acoustics, the resonances of various woods and strings, and other givens of creation. It follows, then, that we cannot say that certain instruments made of those materials are "Christian" and others "non-Christian." And although it may seem too obvious for some, let us also state that Christians won't use different notes or chords or resolve them differently than unbelievers do.

In addition, Christians composing music who are seeking to write aesthetically good music do not necessarily come up with a different style. J. S. Bach, for instance, often held up as a pre-eminent model of the Christian musician, worked within the style of his time, albeit bringing it to new heights of refinement and richness. At the present time, "Christian music" is a term in common use, but it is more likely a style category than a final determination of Christian musical standards. The term "Christian music" is usually applied to music with Christian lyrics in a popular style, a style that began in an effort to provide an alternative to the lyrics of popular music. "CCM [Christian Contemporary Music] came into being when artists and executives took the traditional themes found in church music (evangelism, worship, and ministry) and placed them in music with a contemporary sound. This model legitimized for the church the use of 'secular' popular styles, whether light rock or heavy metal."[34] The CCM musical style itself is thus derived from commercial popular music; the music itself is not in a unique, specifically "Christian" style. This situation is true of any musical style: we do not achieve a uniquely Christian musical style simply by grafting Christian lyrics onto a style of any type. The presence of explicitly Christian lyrics says something about the *lyrics*; it does not necessarily say anything about the *music*.

Those who do assume that "Christian music" exists only in the lyrics soon encounter a dilemma: how to understand music without explicitly Christian lyrics. For instance, a number of years ago, a new album by a well-known artist who is a Christian drew fresh attention to the dilemma. Describing the situation, William Romanowski wrote in *Christianity Today* that although some praised this album,

> a music buyer for religious stores countered, "It's not a Christian album. A Christian album should be clear on the person of Christ, and these lyrics are not." Trying to avoid confusion (or perhaps deflect criticism) concerning the album, a CCM notice alerted religious radio programmers: "As far as the lyrical content is concerned, there's no evangelical bent, no mention of God. If the music you play has to have either of those two elements, you might not want to play it."[35]

The discussion about this album could be more a matter of niche marketing than of Christian aesthetics; but it also reveals a very limited understanding of music. What is especially troubling to me in this situation is the apparent equation that Christian music equals explicit Christian lyrics.

In addition, trying to make all music have an explicit evangelistic statement not only narrowly limits the under-

---

34 William Romanowski, "Where's the Gospel?" *Christianity Today*, 41:14 (December 8, 1997): 44.

35 Romanowski, 44.

standing of the musician's task, but can also result in both gimmicky composition and a manipulative use of music.[36] When we understand creation and our task in it aright, we can see that our task in music is much more wide-ranging and comprehensive. One writer recognizing the range of our task is Charlie Peacock, a veteran songwriter and producer of CCM. "'The contemporary Christian music community must begin to write music and lyrics from a kingdom perspective,' writes Peacock. He means that Christian songs should not only be about Jesus and salvation but also 'all of creation,' including such supposedly 'worldly' topics as romantic love. Only in this way can Christian music demonstrate 'the lordship of Christ over all of life.'"[37]

Our task does include composing and performing songs specifically about God and his works and our relationship to him, music for worship, music to express our penitence, music to celebrate redemption. "Music can have a thoroughly Christian calling to bear the good news with special grace and to bear the bad news of sin and estrangement with shattering power."[38] But our task allows also for singing about a wide range of human experiences, human joys, societal sorrows, and community occasions. It allows for us to sing lullabies, and songs for weddings, as the heading for Psalm 45 indicates. It allows for Old Testament musicians to sing in time of war,[39] and for Leslie Bassett, a Christian composer, to write *Collect*, an anthem of penitence sung against a recording of the sounds

---

36 "Music and the Witnessing Church," Ch. 10 of Harold Best's *Music Through the Eyes of Faith* (San Francisco: Harper San Francisco, 1993) presents helpful insights into "witness music."

37 Chris Lutes, "What Makes Music 'Christian'?" *Christianity Today* 43:7 (June 14, 1999): 86.

38 Frank Burch Brown, *Good Taste, Bad Taste, and Christian Taste: Aesthetics in religious life* (Oxford: Oxford University Press, 2000), 7.

39 2 Chronicles 20:21.

of war. It allows for J. S. Bach, a Christian composer, to write the *Peasant Cantata* about country life. And our task allows for writing and performing music without any words at all. Christians can dance to music that is simply for dancing – no need for any text at all. Christians may and should write and perform pieces without deliberate programmatic[40] intent such as piano sonatas, guitar solos, orchestral symphonies; these forms too care for and develop the creation. The Christian's legitimate scope in music is very wide.

May we use music written or performed by non-Christians?

What about music written or performed by non-Christians? To repeat, unbelievers are gifted to compose and perform excellent music that does indeed nourish us and help us to grow aesthetically. We may indeed use and enjoy such music, giving thanks to God for the gifts he poured out on these musicians.[41] In fact, the problem with using and enjoying music by non-Christians might not be the use and the enjoyment, but instead a failure to recognize the source of these gifts and to give gratitude to the Giver. Because the handiwork is not the maker, we can enjoy the good music of a non-Christian while at the same time not accepting misdirection or unbelief or immorality in the life of that person (or in our own).

If, however, using this music is a stumbling block to any

---

40 "Programmatic" here refers to the musical meaning, not of being on a concert program, but of having "a program" or intentional non-music reference, i.e., a related story or nonmusical depiction.

41 "If we regard the Spirit of God as the sole fountain of truth, we shall neither reject the truth itself, nor despise it wherever it shall appear, unless we wish to dishonor the Spirit of God. . . . But shall we count anything praiseworthy or noble without recognizing at the same time that it comes from God?" John Calvin, *Institutes of the Christian Religion*, ed. John T. McNeill, trans. Ford Lewis Battles (Philadelphia: Westminster, 1960), II.2.16, quoted in Bolt, 50.

Christian, that person should not use it. Sometimes the associations with certain kinds of music (the lifestyles of the musicians, the venue of the music, etc.) are such that it would be wise to distance ourselves from them. That is a matter of individual and/or collective judgment and wisdom. A few examples illustrate. During the 1930's in the United States the locale in which jazz was often played – brothels and speak-easies, often sponsored by the Mafia – considerably tainted the image of jazz. Decent people did not frequent those places; by implication, it was assumed that decent people did not listen to or play jazz, and even that jazz was non-Christian. As the associations fell away, however, it became evident that the music of jazz itself – the actual notes and style of Dixieland, for instance – do not necessarily mean prostitution, drunkenness, or crime; jazz has come to be judged by musical, aesthetic standards. In our own time we need to make a similar distinction about rock and rap music, discriminating between the context in which rock is played and the musical value in the music itself. Whenever the Gospel comes to a new cultural area of the world, the dilemma is faced anew. Some new Christians might want to disassociate themselves from an indigenous style of music that is associated with their former paganism. Others might wish to use a style of music indigenous to them but in a new and believing context. We need to discern what is inherent in the music and what is in the associations of the music.

How do intentions fit in?

Then there is the matter of intentions. Whether with texted or non-texted music, intentions do count. We find them expressed in a variety of ways – the prayer of dedication before the choral concert, the stated intention of the CCM artist who "just wants to praise the Lord," and the notations of J.S.

Bach, who wrote at the start of each composition *Jesu, juva* (Jesus, help) and at the conclusion, *Soli Deo gloria* (to God alone be the glory). The attitude of the heart and the intention of the will are indeed critical. Without them, our finest music is in God's ears but a noisy gong and a tinny cymbal.

But how those intentions play out is also of critical importance in the content of the music – the "what" and the "where" and the "how" of the music. It figures in the content – in what happens between the *Jesu juve* and the *Soli Deo gloria*. It is important that the singer in church be sincere in his musical offering; it is also important he choose a well-crafted and appropriate piece and sing it in tune. It is important that the composer wishes to honor God with her compositions; it is also important that she use, for instance, good harmonic craftsmanship and write well-shaped lines.

Our intention to serve God will influence not only the content but also the venue of the music, not only what we do but also where we do it. And the playing out of that intention will have a wide and various scope. As we seek to care for our neighbor in music, we recognize that the lordship of Christ over all makes every area of life an appropriate neighborhood for service. A musician need neither scorn local service, nor fear the professional "big time." The intention to serve may lead a musician to seek service in the Boston Symphony Orchestra or in a small Dakota town, in a school or a concert stage or a film studio. All these areas – local, national, even international – are valid arenas of Christian service. The neighbors we serve may be the audience in Carnegie Hall or the child in our care, the worshippers in a church or the children in an elementary school, the students at a small college or those attending a great university. All are worthy of our musical care.

And the intention will also influence *how* we do it. We

will seek in all matters musical to serve our neighbor, from the conduct in our rehearsals to the disciplined use of our practice time to the attitude of service in the selection of concert material thoughtfully chosen both to delight and to stretch the listeners.

Our intention to serve God encompasses all of these – the "what," the "where," and the "how," which are all part of our spiritual service. "Human life in all its aspects is a thoroughly spiritual affair," writes Albert Wolters.[42] In professional as well as in private life, in cultural enterprises as well as in moral behavior, and in the content and conduct of all of them, we are to seek spiritual wisdom and understanding – to develop spiritual discernment! – and claim God's promise to guide us.

Can music make us sin or believe?

Music can be powerfully moving. Its intricate connection with emotions is a topic for essays other than this one. However, we can discuss briefly here the limits of music's power. Because music is emotionally moving, some fear that it will influence us to evil. Parents fear that rock and rap will lead their children into immoral behavior and rebellious attitudes. Others hope that through music, they can influence others to certain actions or beliefs. Advertisers believe or at least hope that the tunes in commercials will be influential in selling their product. Some evangelists believe or at least hope that the right music will put people in a "mood" for worship and help them come to Christ. Can it actually do so?

We can be helped by our understanding that music is a creaturely activity, something made by humans. Thus, although it can be influential and moving, it is not a supernatural power; music is not a magic. Music is influential, but it is not irresistible. And thus its power to influence falls into

---

42 Wolters, 35. See 34–35 for a thoughtful discussion of spiritual discernment.

the realm of our choice-making. We cannot blame our sins on the music! Music can neither "make" us sin nor "make" us purchase a given brand of soap.

Similarly, music does not have the power to "make" us believe. Only the Holy Spirit has that power! Planners of music for worship and evangelistic events should take heed of the limits of music. Selecting music to express the service and move the listener is one thing; seeking music in hope of manipulating the hearer is quite another.

At the same time, however, we recognize that people can be influenced by music, even powerfully. Its potency is well-known by every film-maker who plans the ominous music to maximize our terror during the scary scenes! Just as we are well-advised to select our movies with care, so must we be discerning about music. If listening to certain songs encourages our vulnerability to think greedy or lascivious thoughts or to love mediocrity, responsible action on our part includes putting those songs out of earshot. Even though music is not a supernatural magic, it, like other cultural products, can influence us. Music contributes to a culture; and culture, directed toward or against God, serves to shape us. We are responsible for the music we choose to listen to, and also that which we choose to present to other listeners.

How does music carry "meaning"?

What music means, or better, how music carries meaning, is a multilayered issue. A thorough discussion of this intricate matter is not possible in these pages; but an overview of the topic from a musician's point of view is in order, partly because musicians are often faced with the question. In discussing the meaning of music, we must be careful neither to discern too little meaning in music, nor to attribute too much. On the one hand, many would protest limiting the meaning of music to being merely sensory pleasure; but to search music for its meaning as if music exists as a code for the purpose of carrying verbal messages or "propositional truth" asks music to "mean" in ways it is not intended to "mean." How then shall we understand this matter? The discussion here will name, though surely not exhaust, some principal issues and proceed to the central and critical issue, which is an understanding of how music means.

Even the word "meaning" means different things to different people. One issue in the discussion is whether we can even say a piece of music has a generally-agreed-upon meaning. For often when people talk about the meaning of a piece of music, what they really mean is what the piece means to themselves. And there's no doubt that the significance of a piece may be very personal indeed; the piece in question may have been played at our wedding, or attached to a favorite family moment that we treasure in memory, or, without any particular associations, "mean a lot" to us. Such *personal significance* is valid and important; it is a different matter, however, than a *generally-agreed-upon meaning*. That's a distinction worth noting, especially in this post-modern age, when the meaning of anything is sometimes construed as merely relative to the individual.

Another issue in the discussion is whether the meaning of a piece of music is contained entirely within the piece of music itself, or whether the context of the music must be included in a consideration of its meaning. Certainly one way in which music carries meaning is by association, the associations being not individual but generally held. We associate a certain piece by Mendelssohn with weddings and another by Elgar with graduation ceremonies, because those are the occasions on which we commonly hear these pieces. The associations may even come about long after its composition. Some of the "sacred" and "secular" meanings attributed to music are not inherent in the music but accrue to it by association. We associate "Christian values" with a given tune because we sing it with Christian words or hear it in church; we associate "secular" values with a given tune because we hear it on a concert stage or in a pub. We associate "pagan values" with given musical materials because the culture out of which they come was originally pagan. Music easily picks up meaning from its context. It is important, therefore, to distinguish internal meaning in music from meaning by association. For when original associations fall away, our perception of the "meaning" of the music can shift.

On the other hand, at times the occasion or social context of the music may be more inextricably connected with its meaning, or may influence our understanding of its meaning. In such situations, understanding the context may be important to understanding the music. In fact, well-crafted music does show a correlation between the materials and shape of the music and the use and purpose of the music or the text, if there is one. Though context may help shape a composition, the piece may not depend on that context for meaning. And in time the contextual associations may fall away, leaving the meaning of the music to be understood in solely musical terms.

Yet another issue is whether and to what extent the worldview of the composer is discernible in the music. Going to creation is again instructive. We can learn from God's handiwork, from the trees and mountains, petunias and polar bears, that there is a God, that he is someone with power and imagination, and that he is to be acknowledged and worshipped. But we cannot learn from creation about God in his entirety, cannot learn his plan of salvation in Jesus Christ. To learn those things we must go to his Word, to the Scriptures, and to Jesus Christ Incarnate. Similarly, a piece of music is the handiwork of some person; the piece of music can tell us of the existence of a composer or performer and something of his style and skill, but it may not unequivocally convey his worldview; for that we must talk with the person or read his specific statements. Often, rather than formulating a judgment from a single piece or two, we must patiently review a broad segment of a musician's work, spread over years or even a lifetime, to formulate a reliable judgment about his intentions and worldview. Of course, a musician's own statements about his work help to clarify his intentions and views; they should be both sought and encouraged. And any such study must also include a consideration of whether and to what extent the worldview of the composer is suspended or altered or tempered by the performer.

In addition, musicians (and listeners, too) are informed not only by their own worldview, but also influenced by the spirits and the styles of their time. The correlations and influences may be dramatic and obvious, but they may also be subtle or obscure. The precise interaction of spirit, worldview, and person of the musician in a piece of music is so complex as to make us cautious about quick or hard and fast judgments. Still, discovering the correlations and distinguishing the influences are important tasks in which we should seek to develop discernment. Such discernment, however, is not gained quickly or through a surface assessment, but is developed through careful and thoughtful study of cultural and musical history and of musical structure, as well as through sensitive listening.

Even as we develop that discernment, even as we seek to "test the spirits," in music as in all cultural products, let us avoid considering discerning of the spirit of the age or the worldview of the musician to be the *only* task in understanding the music. Wolterstorff writes,

> distortion will result if we take as the basic framework of our approach to art, this phenomenon of the work's being an expression of the world behind it. . . . [T]here will of course be an important relation between the work and the convictions or concerns of the artist. . . . But to focus just on this relation of work to consciousness of artist is to overlook all the rest of the rich embeddedness of art in the life of mankind. If this is all one attends to, an extremely truncated, reduced understanding of the arts will result.[43]

When we do consider the music itself, as discrete as it can be from its context and as a musical art rather than as a code for verbal messages, we need to note that music does not carry meaning in the same way and with the same clarity that other arts do or that anything with text does. (I have been writing here of music as music; any text or lyrics associated with the music of course affects the meaning.) For the meaning of music is primarily *musical*, not conceptual; a melody or a chord progression is not capable of carrying a specific conceptual meaning as can a poem or story or, even more, an essay.

Music means in *musical* ways. Music cannot be contained in words, or translated into words. Music is not a substitute for verbal language. It operates in its own way in its own sphere, which is different from other spheres of communication. The symphonic music of Brahms, the fiddle tunes of Appalachia, pieces of Dixieland jazz all communicate a great deal, all "say" a lot; but if we try to sum it up in a proposition, we have missed the point. Words are indeed one thing we have to work with when we are trying to communicate with each other about music (as these words attest!). But music cannot be reduced to words. In fact, when musicians try to communicate with each other about music, they often do not use words at all; they use music – they sing or play. Words can help us; they can point us toward perception and understand-

---

43 Wolterstorff, 89–90.

ing, but they cannot capture the whole of music, for it is a musical, not a verbal art.

How, then, does music mean? How can we learn to understand its *musical* meanings? We can learn to "read" the musical meanings mostly by listening to a great deal of music, aware, of course, that the musical conventions through which music communicates can vary with the style and the culture. Musical meanings arise from the choice and the relationships of the musical materials – the rhythms, tone colors, melodic shapes. For example, chromatically descending melodies and dark tone colors can be understood in a purely musical way. These musically drooping gestures can also connect with the words and emotions of sorrow. Boldly leaping figures, ascending, and bright tone colors can be understood in entirely musical terms as well. They also fit well with texts and emotions of exuberance and joy. I hesitate to say that these musical gestures "mean" sorrow or joy, because their "meanings" are musical. However, there is a certain fittingness between the musical and nonmusical qualities involved. In addition, the "musical meaning" of a musical gesture can connect well with a variety of textual or pictorial "meanings." One example that comes to mind is the action of fast motoric rhythms in steady note values, which by themselves, musically, communicate musical energy and drive. Such rhythms do not have to connect with a "meaning" outside of the music. But they can, and they have; those motoric rhythms, connected with circling melodic motifs, have been used to picture a train (as in Honegger's *Pacific 231*) and a spinning wheel (as in Schubert's *Gretchan am Spinnrade*) and even frantic running from God (as in Ken Medema's *See How They Run*).[44]

The correlation between musical implications and non-

---

44 See Wolterstorff (96–110) for an intriguing discussion of fittingness within and between diverse realms of reality.

musical meanings is used consciously and deliberately when a piece has what musicians call a "program" – the intentional effort to "picture" a place or character or story in music. "Program music" has no words, but by means of the title or program notes informs us of the item being pictured. Through the composer's choice of rhythm and melody, we do imagine the thing being pictured in music – a sunrise over the Grand Canyon for instance, or chickens pecking inside their shells, or a train. The still rhythm, the high shimmer of violins, the flute flutters in Grofe's *Grand Canyon Suite* call forth an image of morning over a vast space where the only motion is that of the sun a-rising and the birds singing. The erratic staccato rhythms in Mussorgsky's "Ballet of the Unhatched Chicks" from *Pictures at An Exhibition* stimulate our imagination of what we ourselves might never have seen, the pecking of hatching chicks.

So the way music means musically permits program music. Similarly, musical meanings coordinate with our emotions – loud and busy pieces coordinate with our adrenalin-enhanced activity in joyful situations, quiet melodies of small range in gentle tone colors fit tranquil emotions. When we are "moved" by music, we are likely moved to or with a *musical* emotion, a musical emotion that fits well with personal emotions, in a subtle fit between musical and psychological realms akin to that of musical meaning and pictorial details.

The music-pictures of program music are exciting, and the connection of musical emotion to personal or psychological emotion subtle and rich. But a few caveats are in order. First, music does not *depend* on picturing for its success; even without knowing the intended "picture," we can understand and enjoy the piece *musically*. Also, and importantly, not all music has or needs or should have a "program": music's "meaning" and its ability to communicate is in musical, not pictorial or verbal terms. We do it a disservice to expect of it other than what it is.[45]

Also, it should be noted that the musical meaning of a piece is not necessarily universally understood. The Brahms symphony or a piece of Dixieland may not immediately communicate to an audience in Tibet that is unfamiliar with the specific musical implications and realizations in Western symphonic music and jazz; neither will the music of those Tibetans immediately communicate to a person in the American Great Plains, who does not know the musical conventions and their musical implications in Oriental music. Music is indeed a universal experience, but it is not one universal "language."

All these nuances of meaning are embedded in an overarching understanding of creation. As a human response in sound in and to God's creation, music has meaning because it is part of God's creation, a world God has infused with meaning.

How do we evaluate music?
Where do the standards come from?

If, then, music is an area of life for discernment as well as for pleasure, how shall we evaluate it? If the main criterion for music is not whether it can be classified as "Christian" or not, what are the standards for evaluation? Is music to be evaluated by the internal quality of the music itself or by the direction of the musicians' hearts or both? Of what does good quality in the music itself consist?[46] How do we perceive goodness and

---

45 For an exercise in perceiving meaning in specific pieces, see Munson and Drake, 83–100.

46 Concepts of craftsmanship, imagination, expressiveness, and fittingness are developed richly by Nicholas Wolterstorff in "The Given with which the Artist Works," Part 3, Chapter 2 of *Art in Action*. Harold Best's *Music Through the Eyes of Faith* further addresses issues of quality in music. See also "On Musical Excellence" by Karen DeMol (1992), for a more elaborate presenta-

weakness, quality and mediocrity in music? And where do we get our standards?

Some may say that the only criterion is one's personal taste: all that matters is my own personal preference. In this statement, taste is synonymous with preference – my individual likes and dislikes. Certainly we all do have our personal musical preferences. But we cannot claim that this ends the discussion, even though and even when our musical preferences are close to our hearts. In *evaluating* music, in seeking to discern its quality, the first question is not, "Do I like it?"

For, first of all, our personal taste is based on *something*. Often that "something" is familiarity; what we *like* is what is *familiar*, and we can become persuaded that whatever is familiar is good. Our taste is then limited to what we already know. Also, deciding what we like involves some degree of perceiving the music, of enjoying or not enjoying it, and as a consequence making a judgment. That being so, our taste is related to our ability to perceive, to our musical perception skills, even to our experience – none of which is absolute. Our taste may be individual, but it is not indisputable.[47]

Note that personal taste is not the criterion in other areas of life. In areas of life with aesthetic dimensions, such as writing, visual art, graphic design, architecture, personal dress, we acknowledge that though we have personal preferences, there are and should be principles of design, balance, and appropriateness at work both in creating and in evaluating these expressions. Personal preference is not the sole criterion for areas of life outside the arts, either. Take dining, for instance, in which "taste" is literal. I may prefer cookies, chips, and pop to green beans and oranges, and I may even choose to

---

tion of the material in this section.

47 Brown, 10. See also pages 13–23 for an insightful discussion of perceiving, appreciating, and appraising. See also Calvin Seerveld, *Normative Aesthetics* (Sioux Center: Dordt College Press, 2014), 127–133.

limit myself to sugary and salty foods. But I doubt that any of us would claim this to be a good choice, a healthy choice. I would draw your rightful disagreement if I claimed it was. Further, if I do limit myself to cookies, chips, and pop, I will lose my ability to enjoy the good taste of apples and avocados – I will not like them. My taste will need to be retrained through exposure to healthy foods. Though we might hate to admit it, our taste in the arts may be uninformed. We are not born with good taste, but we can develop aesthetically sound musical tastes through training.

But is not music different than food in regard to taste and even "nourishment"? No. We who believe that all areas of life belong to the Lord, in a world we believe to be God's, and in which good, mediocre, and poor exist in all arenas and endeavors, we are to be wise in all our choices, including aesthetic choices. Acknowledging this is not a call to elitism, but an invitation to open ourselves to growth.

Our musical perceptions and our imaginations require training, which may strike us as wearisome and tedious. Learning discernment requires humility – acknowledging that we do not know everything. Refusing to open ourselves to such training prevents us from perceiving the glory of God's creation as developed and expressed in art and music.[48] But if we make the effort and in humility open our ears and imaginations to such training, we may be surprised to find that enjoyment has crept in, deep and rich.[49]

So if personal preference is not the criterion, what is?

In advancing criteria for excellence, I am assuming that the pursuit of excellence is worthy. The Bible certainly is not shy about excellence. The building of the tabernacle, for ex-

---

48 Ken Meyers, "Introduction" to Munson and Drake.

49 "We are not born aesthetically wise. It is something we must learn through diligent study and repentance" (Munson and Drake, 29).

ample, was entrusted to the gifted and the skilled (Exodus 26:1; 35:30–36:1). The training of the musicians in the Old Testament Israelite community was specific and demanding and under the direction of head musicians (1 Chronicles 6:31–42; 16:3–6, 42). The New Testament even charges us to think about those things that are lovely, excellent, and of good report (Philippians 4:8).

In all our concerns, we should always look first to the Bible. Here, however, we do not find directions for the actual notes of music. The Bible does not tell us which chord to use, or what makes a good melody, or what scales are ordained, or how many steps should be in an octave. What we find is our understanding of the foundation of music in creation and of music as a part of all of life. Here we find general admonitions to quality. Here we find norms for our attitude and for the use of music (and everything else) for the building of the body of believers. And here we get our concept of who we are, what kind of world our music is part of, and whose world it is. But the Bible does not help us in choosing specific notes.

Then we look to God's other revelation, the Creation. In the natural world we find no inherent music that could serve as model.[50] We could infer some general principles about variety and about the union of form and function. Some people, in fact, have worked at finding aesthetic principles in the natural world, but find it easier to do so in terms of the visual arts. To my knowledge, they have not yet found specific musical guidelines.

From what, then, do we derive our guidelines for actual musical composition and performance?[51] A general norm for

---

50 There are bird songs, of course; but although they are a sort of incipient music, I have not yet found a generally-accepted aesthetic of human music based on them; the work of Olivier Messaien notwithstanding.

51 "God's ordinances for our life in culture and society 'can only be uncovered by man through experience and investigation. Whoever desires to under-

all the arts is imaginativity, which in music finds its expression in sound. More specific norms for composition come from the art of music itself.[52] Common general standards for all music include craftsmanship; unity and variety; aesthetic expressiveness; integratedness of materials, shape, and use; and authenticity, all of which apply in a rich variety of national, historical, and cultural styles. Of these, let us here consider especially three: craftsmanship, expressiveness, and the integrity of materials and function. These criteria apply to all musics, be they high art music, folk, or popular. Let us also consider standards for our attitude toward and use of music.

Technique or craftsmanship: To evaluate music, we

---

stand nature must study nature; whoever wants to be a farmer must actually engage in farming; whoever wants to be a salesman must get busy in commerce, etc. It is not the study of Scripture but careful investigation of what God teaches us in his creation and providence that equips us properly for these tasks" (Herman Bavinck, cited by Bolt, 119).

52 *In Rainbows for a Fallen World*, Calvin Seerveld writes: "When you want to find out how God ordered plants to grow, you don't go study the synoptic Gospels: you go examine plants with a sharp knife and microscope. If you need to discover what chinks in a person's emotional makeup are apt to crack wide open in later life and how you should put an arm around such a one to help hold them together so they can heal, you don't go read Proverbs for details on neuroses and psychoses: you study the case histories of emotionally disturbed people and examine others who display psychic health, make notes, reflect, and bite your fingernails as psychotherapist lest you mess up the life of somebody Christ died for. If you must decide, so you can give leadership, on whether Chagall's stained glass window honouring the late Mayor Daley in the Art Institute of Chicago is more or less significant than the striking piece by Abraham Rattner that takes a whole wall of the downtown loop synagogue, you don't go read Paul's letters, the Psalms, or even Isaiah 40 to look for information on 'beauty': instead, you go study the art for hours, learn the composer or artist's whole oeuvre to get context, examine the history of music, memorial and cult artistry, take a considered stand on the nature of art and slowly begin to discern what counts. All of this scrutiny is exceedingly difficult, because cultural artefacts complicate creation by slipping in also the committed slant of a man or woman's heart; but you make, perhaps in a communion with others, an aesthetic judgment that will bring relative blessing or a curse to those whom it influences" (13–14).

consider technique. In performance, in Western music, good technique includes getting all the pitches correct and playing them in tune, with reliable rhythm, and with good articulation. Good technique includes appropriate and rich tone quality and requires an understanding of style. As we become more advanced, technique becomes more multi-layered. It calls for scholarly insight, so that we play not only on a good instrument, but also on an instrument appropriate to the style or historical period of the music or the ethnic origin of the folk tune; not only with a balanced orchestra, but with a historically appropriate size of orchestra; not only in tune, but also according to the tuning system of that time or that style, be it the blues or fifteenth-century lute music.

In composition, technique is better called craftsmanship. Good craftsmanship includes consistency in the handling of the musical materials (the themes, harmonies, rhythms). Craftsmanship includes observing the specific compositional practices associated with the style chosen. For example, in certain classical Western styles, composers avoid parallel fifths, particular note doublings, and bumpy chord connections. In jazz, composers handle scales in particular ways. In any style, craftsmanship includes writing within the capabilities of the instruments chosen, even writing idiomatically for them. In any style good craftsmanship requires composing with a coherence of materials.

Then there are technological accompaniments: the instruments themselves are well-made and are in tune, the performance space – hall, church, room – is acoustically alive and balanced, the sound system, if used, is working, of good quality and monitored carefully, and the recording technology and equipment are of fine quality.

So good quality in music consists of good craftsmanship, good technique. But not only of that.

Expressiveness: To evaluate music, we also consider expressiveness. Excellence is not only getting all the correct notes. We have all heard flawless performances that are wooden and have sensed that something essential to music was missing; what is needed is expressiveness. Excellence is not merely technical perfection. In fact, in these modern times we should beware of buying into a false understanding of perfection from the recording industry, which by "patching" can insert corrections into the recording, thus achieving a flawlessness rarely possible in live music-making. In fact, while a certain amount of proficiency is foundational to expressiveness, technique does not have to be flawless before expressiveness can begin.

There is wisdom for us in a story related by William Edgar:

> When the great pianist Artur Schnabel finished his monumental recordings of the complete Beethoven sonatas, the studio engineer came to him and explained that there had been a number of mistakes here and there. If Schnabel would come down to the studio he could play these measures and they could be dubbed in. Schnabel refused the offer. He even offered to do the entire thirty-two sonatas again, incorporating whatever new mistakes might be involved! But under no circumstances would he allow the studio to spoil the unity of the original performance with the mood and ambiance he had created.[53]

What is expressiveness? Here words falter while examples would flourish. However, we can say briefly that in performance, expressiveness is knowing, after getting all the notes in tune, when to bend a pitch, and how much, and why. It is knowing how much to move a yearning note upward, how far to flat a blue note. It is knowing, after getting all the rhythms metronomically correct, when to stretch a note, and how much, and why. It is knowing how to shape a melody. It is not only accurate but also sensitive timing. It is that moment in

---

53 Edgar, 14.

a recent rehearsal of the orchestra I play in, a rehearsal when we were all preoccupied with not getting lost in the first read-through of a challenging new piece, when a trumpet player shaped a soft solo with such lovely delicacy that we all sensed a unique and essential quality in the passage.

In composition, expressiveness is nuance, subtlety. It is suggestiveness, shape. It is the choice of all the right materials at a given moment to achieve the desired musical effect.

It is the expressive aspect of music that aestheticians try to capture and explain – confined, again, to words. Calvin Seerveld says it is allusiveness, suggestiveness. William Edgar calls it "metaphor," signifying a way of experiencing time and space.[54] It is perhaps the aspect of music that most strongly relates to our sense of imagination.

Though difficult to define in words, expressiveness is at the aesthetic heart of that shaping of sound we call music. We assert this while at the same time acknowledging the role of function (for dance or liturgy or celebration), the connection to emotion (music to express or correlate with our deep feelings), the importance of textual content, and the political, social, and sociological implications and context of music. The aesthetic is central. Even when music is present in a situation where the emphasis is on something else, the aesthetic is paramount. Music may have a didactic purpose: we may find or devise a tune to help us remember the letters of the alphabet or the books of the Bible or the names of Jesus' disciples or the directions for sailing across the Pacific; but if that tune is not aesthetically rich, we will have a good mnemonic device but not good music. Music may have a liturgical or ceremonial purpose; but even if the music enables all the graduates or the bridesmaids to walk in step, or the skaters to stay together, or the congregation to proclaim the words of a Psalm together,

---

54 Seerveld, 105; Edgar, Ch. 3.

if the music is not aesthetically rich, we will not have good music. Music may have emotional significance, expressing our joy, loneliness, or grief, or may effectively serve a political purpose and unite the patriots of a cause or a country; but if the music itself is not aesthetically rich, we will not have good music. Even when we write or choose music to carry a Christian text, we need musical expressiveness. For if the music isn't aesthetically good, we may as well dispense with it and use a fine poem or a speech instead.

Because expressiveness is difficult to capture in words, we "catch" the idea more than we are taught it. Performers catch it from great performers, teachers, and artists who model and instruct. Listeners both to familiar and new music learn to discern it under the tutelage of those with an ear to hear. We learn quality in musical expressiveness not from a lecture, but from exposure to good music, under the tutelage and/or encouragement of an expert in the field. One needs a teacher or guide who says, "Listen to this now. Hear how the little twist in the melody here fits the hidden suggestion in the text, or sets us up for the next section, or keeps the harmony the same yet different. Here right now, in this piece, this is evidence of expressiveness." And by discerning the same in numerous different instances, we build up a sense of expressiveness and become sensitive to pieces and performances that are both well-crafted and richly expressive. We begin to distinguish them from those that are well-crafted but devoid of expressiveness, from those whose craftsmanship is flawed and yet are expressive, and from those that are both shoddy and soulless.

Because this tutelage, this entry into the perception of musical quality, is best guided by an insider in a style, requires musical examples, and takes considerable time, these paragraphs cannot articulate much further what creates aesthetic expressiveness. However, all of us are encouraged and challenged to embark on the journey of learning, starting wherever we are, and moving to understand, discern, and appreciate musical quality ever more deeply. Through this journey, by listening to good music that rewards repeated listening, we become familiar with and develop a taste for good music; we may find that through these efforts, we are rewarded with a richer enjoyment of music.

Technical excellence and musical expressiveness are criteria that exist for music in all styles and at all levels. Of course, what can be achieved by a mature professional, technically and expressively, is at a different level than that of a student. We do take note of varying levels of achievement. We acknowledge a sort of absolute or ideal excellence: the finest compositions performed with outstanding technique and superb artistic expressiveness. It is the best that has yet been done, the best that can be done. This excellence is an ideal, a goal, a destination. We would admit that this being the limited and imperfect world that it is, the highest level of excellence experienced in our world is still not the best possible, the best that we will experience in the new heaven and the new earth. As the poet Stanley Wiersma once wrote: In this world, "it sounds as though we expect A+ from [our] life, when all we have ever achieved is a C."[55]

We also acknowledge a relative excellence, as appropriate, for example, for students at various stages of development, even for styles still in the making. If when judging a junior high festival I were to hold to standards of absolute excellence, I would give everyone a "poor" rating. Instead I use a standard of excellence related to what younger adolescents are capable of. This excellence is a way-station on the road of excellence, a point on an infinite line. We appropriately encourage growth, even press for it, for both musicians and listeners. "Good enough at this level" should not stall out at "good enough." It

---

55 Stanley Wiersma, *Adjoining Fields* (Grand Rapids: English Department of Calvin College, 1987), 33.

is appropriate to expect those junior high students, four years later, to have reached a different level. However, perceiving the appropriate level of excellence one may expect in each situation is a task requiring not only fine musical sensitivity but also great pastoral skill and wisdom. Our conception of excellence thus includes a sense both of the ideal, the best possible, and of a point of development, both destination and journey.

Given these criteria of technical and expressive excellence, one might well ask if only certain styles qualify as excellent. The exploration and development of sound has resulted in a multiplicity of musical styles, a diversity that is legitimate and rich. But are some of these styles capable of greater aesthetic richness? The concept of relative excellence applies here: some styles can lend themselves to a higher level of excellence than others. It is possible and appropriate to say that two pieces of music are each excellent among their kind, but that one style is capable of a higher, broader, or deeper level of craftsmanship or expressiveness. It could be considered whether there are ceilings on what we can expect in the compositional quality of certain styles, of Christian Contemporary, for instance, or rock, or even classical. It could also be debated whether certain styles only appear to be limited, until later or better masters show the higher quality of which they are capable. Was the classical symphony, for example, excellent in the hands of Stamitz and Sammartini, or did it seem to be a musically modest genre only until the masters Haydn and Mozart set their hands to it?

Integrity of musical materials, shape, and function: A third main area of evaluation is in the matching of the music with its intended use or purpose. As noted above, music functions in our lives in a multitude of ways. Music is appropriately used with actions and activities, such as liturgy and dancing. It highlights ceremonies such as weddings, parades, birthdays, and inaugurations. It is a partner of theater and dance. It is used in and for therapy.[56] Music is used for personal things too. Whether or not some "purists" approve, music is used for relaxation. It is used to make work more pleasant and more efficient. It plays a role in entertainment and amusement. And it is used simply, and richly, for listening.

These correlations come in part because music partners well. It is a ready and appropriate companion to many other activities and functions in life. The dimension we call rhythm, that shaping of the time element of creation, goes well with other activities that work in time, such as drama and dancing, parades and processionals. This partnership leads to rhythm's role in celebrations such as graduations and inaugurations. Music can enhance the efficiency and pleasure of work; it even helps to coordinate the motions of those needing to work together in rhythm, as a heritage of sea chanties, railroad songs, and other work songs attests. Its expressiveness partners well with whatever carries emotion, be it funerals or celebrations.

In evaluating music, we must consider how well the music matches that to which it is partnered. How well does the music fit and serve the liturgical action? How well does it help carry the play? Can one march well with the parade music and dance well with the dance music – not *to* it, but *with* it?

If the music is purely for listening, the technique and expressiveness, both in composition and performance, are the principal components. If, however, the music is for an activity or function, it is not only technique and expressiveness that matter, but also how well it fits the situation.[57]

---

56 Dale Topp, in his *Music in the Christian Community* (Grand Rapids: Eerdmans, 1976), presents these "uses" of music in connection with various areas of life: music and serenity (therapy and relaxation); music and friendship; music and declaration (political statement); music and action (liturgy, dance, play); music and amusement (entertainment); music and education (cultural understanding).

57 We note here briefly the question of whether music for a function is inferior or superior to music purely for listening. Some would label art for art's

We need it all. For if we focus only on the function and forget about technical and expressive quality, music becomes only a tool. It is inadequate to claim that as long as the music is functional, it is good, that as long as we can dance to the dance music, or as long as the offertory music matches the time it takes the deacons to pass the plates, or as long as the choir music stirs an audience or congregation to religious feelings, or as long as the advertising ditty sells the product, or as long as people are entertained by the performance, the music "works" and is therefore good. To be good, music should serve its purpose well and at the same time exhibit high musical quality, both technical and expressive.[58] When we say music is poor or mediocre, it may be that it is poorly crafted, or expressively barren, or unsuited to its use, or all of these.

What is excellence in music? As I have summarized elsewhere,[59] excellence is:

superb craftsmanship in composition and
technique in performance
wedded to aesthetic expressiveness
pursued toward the ideal
at the presently appropriate level
together with an integrity of the materials and their shape
with the use for which the music is intended

---

sake elitist or irrelevant, while others consider functional music pedestrian. Wolterstorff reminds us of the role of art as responsible action within all of life. Harold Best reminds us of the instruction in Genesis 2:9, where it is said that the trees God made were "pleasing to the eye and good for food." "Everything that God creates has intrinsic worth, and everything that has worth functions. And He calls this total integration good; beauty, worth, usefulness, and function are united at every turn" (Best, 26). We thus conclude that music for listening is not necessarily "better" than music that accompanies a dance or a worship service.

58 Some writers see Genesis 2:9 as presenting a model for both aesthetic value and usefulness in the arts: "The LORD God made all kinds of trees grow out of the ground – trees that were pleasing to the eye and good for food."

59 Karen De Mol, "On Musical Excellence, *Pro Rege* 20:4 (June, 1992): 10.

undertaken in joyful and obedient response to God's com-mands

> *to develop his good creation of sound*
> *and to serve our neighbors.*

It is important to note that in this discussion of evaluating the music itself, we have not used any terminology about "Christian music," but rather discussed the hallmarks of quality. Richard Wright asserts, "The Creation brings glory to God; its goodness speaks of his goodness, its beauty of his beauty."[60] Our work too, our music, brings glory to God by being good – that is, well-crafted, richly expressive, authentic, and integrated with its function.

Coda

In our engagement with music, both as musicians and as audiences, we need to consider the objective quality of our handiwork – our music – and also the direction and attitude of our hearts. We pursue the components of quality described above not to flaunt our skills or to serve ourselves, but to carry out faithfully and well the tasks of caring for and developing one part of God's world. And we do it with gratitude. Those of us who compose or perform offer up our music to God as worship, in any and all occasions, in the studio and in performance as well as in communal worship. Those of us who listen lift the music we hear to God as an offering as well. In communal worship, those of us in the pew say the "amen" in our hearts to the music of the choir and instruments. In non-liturgical situations, too, such as concerts, those of us who listen can acknowledge and give thanks for the gifts of the Giver as revealed in the skills of the performer and in the craftsmanship of the music.

How then shall we engage in music as part of our lives

---

60 Wright, 170.

as Christians? With gratitude and delight, thankful for God's provision of the materials and his command to be busy with them, and with enjoyment of the good things musicians have made of them. With the attitude of dedicated servants, we are to make, use, and enjoy music in the humble and grateful consciousness that we are God's creatures, at his command caring for and developing his world. We make music to build the Body, as part of neighbor-keeping, to nurture ourselves and others. We make music, use and enjoy music, as delighted stewards of God's marvelous world of sound.

A bibliography of recommended readings

On music

Best, Harold. *Music Through the Eyes of Faith*. San Francisco: HarperSanFrancisco, 1993.

DeMol, Karen. "On Musical Excellence," *Pro Rege* 20:4 (June, 1992).

Edgar, William. *Taking Note of Music*. London: SPCK, 1986.

Johansson, Calvin M. *Music and Ministry: A biblical counterpoint*. Peabody, MA: Hendrickson, 1984.

Schultz, Quentin, et al. *Dancing in the Dark*. Grand Rapids: Eerdmans, 1991.

Topp, Dale. *Music in the Christian Community*. Grand Rapids: Eerdmans, 1976.

On aesthetics and the arts in general

Brand, Hilary, and Adrienne Chaplin. *Art and Soul: Signposts for Christians in the arts*. Carlisle, Cumbria: Solway, 1999.

Brown, Frank Burch. *Good Taste, Bad Taste, and Christian Taste*. Oxford: Oxford University Press, 2000.

Munson, Paul, and Joshua Farris Drake. *Art and Music: A student's guide*. Wheaton: Crossway, 2014.

Rookmaaker, H. R. *Art Needs No Justification*. Downers Grove: Intervarsity Press, 1978.

Ryken, Leland. *The Liberated Imagination*. Wheaton: Harold Shaw Publishers, 1989.

Ryken, Philip Graham. *Art for God's Sake*. Philipsburg, NJ: PR Publishing, 2006.

Seerveld, Calvin. *Rainbows for the Fallen World: Aesthetic life and aesthetic task*. Toronto: Tuppence Press, 1980.

Seerveld, Calvin. *Normative Aesthetics*. Sioux Center: Dordt College Press, 2014.

Wolterstorff, Nicholas. *Art in Action: Toward a Christian aesthetic*. Grand Rapids: Eerdmans, 1980.

On a Reformed/Reformational worldview

Our World Belongs to God: A contemporary testimony. Grand Rapids: CRC Publications, 1986 and 2008.

Bolt, John. *Bavinck on the Christian Life: Following Jesus in faithful service*. Wheaton: Crossway, 2015.

Plantinga, Cornelius, Jr. *Not the Way It's Supposed to Be: A breviary of sin*. Grand Rapids: Eerdmans, 1995.

Walsh, Brian J., and Richard J. Middleton. *The Transforming Vision: Shaping a Christian world view*. Downers Grove: Inter-Varsity, 1984.

Wells, Ronald. *History Through the Eyes of Faith*. San Francisco: Harper and Row, 1993.

Wolters, Albert M. *Creation Regained: Biblical basics for a reformational worldview*, 2nd ed. Grand Rapids: Eerdmans, 2005.

Wright, Richard. *Biology Through the Eyes of Faith*. San Francisco: Harper and Row, 1989.

CPSIA information can be obtained
at www.ICGtesting.com
Printed in the USA
BVHW08s0737250618
519775BV00002B/76/P